Son of DAVID

Stuart Dauermann

Son of DAVID

Healing the Vision of the Messianic Jewish Movement

WIPF & STOCK · Eugene, Oregon

SON OF DAVID
Healing the Vision of the Messianic Jewish Movement

Wipf & Stock
An imprint of Wipf and Stock Publishers
199 W. 8th Avenue, Suite 3
Eugene OR, 97401
www.wipfandstock.com

ISBN 13: 978-1-60899-988-0

www.JourneyToJerusalem.com
www.ShalomTalk.com
info@JourneyToJerusalem.com

Manufactured in the U.S.A.

TABLE OF CONTENTS

I have written this essay on recovering Yeshua's identity as the Son of David because I long for something far greater in and through the Messianic Jewish Movement than what I have seen. Many have almost given up hope that things can get better. I write to share with them a glimmer of light, a spark of newness that just might become a roaring conflagration, burning up the dross, illuminating the darkness, and transforming all we have known. If I succeed in this task, many will join with me, first in acknowledging we are floundering, and then in building on new foundations for a better tomorrow. If I fail, then few if any will be convinced that the present is bleak, or that the future can be brighter than what has been. But if you are in the mood to follow someone carrying a torch into the murk, then come along. I think I have something to show you. For the most part our leaders are dedicated to God. They feel honored to serve him in our context. Yet, if you ask around, you will discover that most feel dissatisfied and frustrated. We want to see great things happen for the honor of the Holy One, but what do we see?

– Stuart Dauermann

THE MESSIANIC JEWISH MOVEMENT: WHAT'S WRONG WITH THIS PICTURE?

Since the late 1960s, the Messianic Jewish Movement has talked about revival—an *act of God*—while too often we have instead seen revivalism—more of *an act*. A movement calling itself the Messianic *Jewish* Movement has increasingly become the Messianic *Jewish-style Movement,* with a decreasing Jewish demographic presence. But what is most telling is that what we are seeing in the Messianic Jewish Movement bears little if any resemblance to what the Bible would lead us to expect: a movement of observant Jews at the heart of the Jewish community, empowered by the Spirit, demonstrating the authority of the risen Messiah—as a sign, demonstration, and catalyst of God's consummating purposes for Israel, the nations, and the entire creation.

Instead, our movement, in varying degrees, is often shaped around the armatures of various forms of sectarian Christianity—either *dispensationalism* (the Missions Movement), or *free-church charismatic* culture (the Congregational Movement). Too often, even in our own eyes, we seem to be pale imitations, or even lapdogs of other communities. And the more one reads the Bible and takes the prophetic word seriously, the more one is forced to recognize that what we are led to expect there is not what we are finding here. What then is the problem?

The answer can be found in the book of Proverbs: "Where there is no vision, the people perish" (29:18 KJV). At the heart of it all, our problem is a lack of integrated vision. The Congregational Movement suffers from *spiritual macular degeneration.*[1] We have lost vision at the center. No wonder we have difficulty driving our movement forward! It is only when we clearly identify that which should be central to our vision that we will be able to get on with a vigorous communal life, discerning and energetically pursuing the purposes of God.

That needed vision will come to us from a deep realization of Yeshua's identity and message. A story from his life is a good place to begin.

Two Blind Men Still Needing to be Healed

Two blind men sitting by the side of the road heard that he was passing by and shouted, "Son of David! Have pity on us!" The crowd scolded them and told them to be quiet, but they shouted all the louder, "Lord! Son of David! Have pity on us!"

Yeshua stopped, called them and said, "What do you want me to do for you?"

They said to him, "Lord, open our eyes."

Filled with tenderness, Yeshua touched their eyes; and instantly they received their sight and followed him (Matt 20:30–34).

We might compare these two blind men to today's church and today's Messianic Jewish Congregational Movement. Each is blind in his own way, but for each the first indication that vision has been restored will be that they will see Yeshua clearly and follow him as never before.

---

1   Macular Degeneration is a progressive eye disease in which the sufferer progressively loses more and more central vision.

Let's look at these two blind communities, first the church and then ourselves. What is each blind to?

The Church Is Blind to the Jewishness of Yeshua

When he told the woman at the well, "we worship what we do know, because salvation comes from the Jews," Yeshua was including himself in the "we" that is the Jewish people (John 4:22). The woman had no difficulty herself identifying him as such, for she said: "How is it that you, a Jew, ask for water from me, a woman of [Samaria]?" (4:9). Although neither Yeshua nor the woman were confused about the matter, a historical survey demonstrates that Yeshua's Jewishness has long been obscured and forgotten.

Examine the church's artistic and literary legacy and you will detect amnesia concerning the Jewishness of Yeshua. Instead, the church embraces a *generic Christ,* the *cosmic Savior,* the *Man for Others,* a *Metaphysical Hero,* a *Chameleon Redeemer* who blends in perfectly wherever he is found. In its paintings, icons, weavings, drawings, and sculptures, the church in every culture makes Jesus over in its own image. You will find the *Gentile Christ* with the aquiline nose, the rugged white *Anglo Saxon Marlboro Man Christ, African and Afro-American Christs, Asian Christs,* often in Buddhist postures of meditative repose, *Indian Christs* looking more Guru than "Jewru," Swinburne's conquering *pale Galilean, Mexican Cristos* twisting in crucified agony, and various *designer Christs,* tailored to fit each consumer culture.

Somehow the church lost sight of what was so obvious to the Samaritan woman: Jesus was, is, and evermore will be a Jew. Healing this blind spot is crucial because the Messiah of faith and the Yeshua of history only intersect in this one who became incarnate in the very Jewish womb of the Virgin Mary. Our faith in the Messiah is groundless wherever we lose contact with his flesh and blood specificity.

Bernard Dupuy saw this clearly in 1974:

> We have to get back to the One who became incarnate
> as a Jew among the Jews; to the One for whom being
> a Jew was not some kind of throw-away garment but
> his very being. . . . It was in becoming incarnate in the
> Jewish people that Jesus offered himself as savior to the
> entire human race. We can acknowledge Jesus only as
> he appeared to us: as this particular Jew, this just and
> suffering servant; it is thus that he reveals himself in order
> to reign over the world.[2]

Yet, no historic creed or confession of the church makes
any reference to Yeshua's Jewishness—not one. *The Man
from Galilee* has become the *Son of Man Without a Country*.
Markus Bockmuehl notes that this substitution was
intentional as a predominantly Gentile church sought to
coalesce its self-definition and legitimacy through distancing
itself and its founder from the Jewish milieu. Certainly, it
was easier for Christians to imagine Christ forsaking the
Jewish people and embracing the church as the new Israel
when they forgot that he remains bone of Jewish bone and
flesh of Jewish flesh.[3]

To be fair, we must note that Bockmuehl also comments
on recent signs of healing in the church. He attributes these
signs to the late 19th- and early 20th-century rebirth of
Christian interest in Jewish studies, to the Holocaust, the
rebirth of the State of Israel, the 1947 discovery of the Dead
Sea Scrolls, and ecumenical breakthroughs of understanding
and bridge-building. Changes in the post-Vatican II Roman
Catholic Church, especially during the reign of John Paul II,

---

2   Bernard Dupuy, "What Meaning Has the Fact that Jesus was Jewish for the
     Christian?" in Hans Kung and Walter Kasper, eds., *Christians and Jews. Concilium:
     Religion in the Seventies, Volume 98*. New York: Seabury, 1974: 74.
3   Marcus Bockmuehl, *Seeing the Word: Refocusing New Testament Study*. Grand
     Rapids: Baker Academic, 2006, 195.

have been the most striking of all.[4] Yet much damage remains to be repaired if the healing of the schism between the Christian and Jewish communions is to be healed.

So much for the church's blindness. What about the Messianic Jewish Congregational Movement?

The Messianic Jewish Movement Is Blind to Yeshua's Office as the Son of David

> The incarnation is not just the union of God and humanity; it is the incarnation of the Son of God in the house of David as the Son of covenant promise. . . . Jesus is not just a man, or generic man; he is that man—that descendant of David.[5]

Twice in his writings, Paul takes pains to point out that Yeshua's *Davidic sonship* is central to the message he himself proclaimed. In Romans 1:2–4, echoing Psalm 2, Paul speaks of "the Good News of God. . . . It concerns his Son—he is descended from David physically; he was powerfully demonstrated to be Son of God spiritually, set apart by his having been resurrected from the dead." And in his second letter to Timothy, Paul adjures him to "Remember Yeshua the Messiah, who was raised from the dead, who was a descendant of David . . . the Good News I proclaim" (2:8).

Yet, in spite of the importance of this theme, its meaning for Messianic Jews today is not talked about. It is not a major agenda item for Messianic Judaism. It is an idea virtually unknown in the workings and worldview of the Messianic Jewish Congregational Movement.

What are the implications of these ideas? What is it that the Messianic Jewish Congregational Movement is missing?

---

4   Ibid., 210–213
5   Craig A. Blaising, "The Future of Israel as a Theological Question." *Journal of the Evangelical Theological Society 44* (no. 3: 435–450), 445.

What does Yeshua's *office* as the Son of David have to do with our present situation?

UNDERSTANDING YESHUA AS THE SON OF DAVID: A CRUCIAL MISSING LINK

Many will protest, perhaps loudly, "But we *do* remember Yeshua is the Son of David! He wouldn't be the Messiah if he were not the Son of David! We always teach this!"

But is that all? Is his being the Son of David simply a matter of lineage, a bit of genetic evidence that he comes from the right family? No.

"Son of David" is Yeshua's office! It names his role as the anointed King whom we are called to serve. Failure to grasp this great truth is a missing link in the Messianic Jewish Movement's understanding its own place in the world. And rather than being something peripheral, it is the blind spot *at the center* of our spiritual macular degeneration.

In the rest of this essay, we will explore Yeshua's *office* as the Son of David, its relationship to the *narratives and covenants* of Scripture, and how we can only *serve* as God's renewal agents within the household of Israel *if and as* our vision of Yeshua as the Son of David is restored. Our blind movement will only see clearly who we are and who we are called to be when we see Yeshua towering over us in this role of roles for the King of Kings.

It helps to begin with the broader story the Bible is telling. The Bible can be seen as a grand narrative, made up of many stories that fit together like a vast mosaic. Looking more closely at these tiles, these stories, helps us better understand where the grand narrative is leading, and the unique role assigned to Yeshua, the Son of David, just as looking more broadly at the grand narrative helps us know better where and how each tile fits.

Biblical Stories and Roles Within Them: *The Chosen, The Also Provided For,* and *The Anti-Chosen*

Elie Wiesel, the brilliant Jewish thinker, reminds us, "God created people because he loves stories."[6] Maybe that's why the Bible has so many of them. Bible scholar Joel Kaminsky points out how the stories in the Tanak frequently involve *the elect,* who receive God's blessing, *the non-elect,* who are blessed along with the elect, and the *anti-elect,* who oppose God and his choices, earning rejection and judgment.[7]

Often, these Bible stories focus on *an elect person* whose relationship with God is the channel of his blessing to *the elect people,* and on *an elect place,* the locale where that blessedness is experienced. Because Kaminsky is concerned to contrast categories with Christian theologizing, he uses the Christian-sounding words *elect* and *election.* I prefer the softer and more Jewish-sounding synonyms, *chosen* and *choice;* and rather than using his term *non-elect,* which sounds so negative, I prefer to speak of *the also-provided-for,* who benefit along with God's chosen ones.

To see how easily these categories apply to Scripture's accounts, consider the story of Joseph. In the Joseph saga, he is *the chosen person,* his father's favorite, and the one who experiences dramatic deliverance through God's intervention. Even after being rejected by his brothers and sent off to Egypt as a slave, Torah reminds us "Adonai was with him; and whatever he did, Adonai prospered" (Gen 39:23). You could not find a more succinct definition of God's provision—his blessing.

God uses Joseph, *the chosen person,* as the means to keep alive the family of Jacob, *the chosen people,* through

---

6   Elie Wiesel, *The Gates of the Forest.* New York: Holt, Rinehart and Winston, 1966, 10.

7   Joel S. Kaminsky, *Yet I Loved Jacob: Reclaiming the Biblical Concept of Election.* Nashville: Abingdon Press, 2007, 10–12.

his administration of a food program growing out of the dreams he interpreted for Pharaoh. The other nations of the area (*the also-provided-for*) were fed and sustained along with Jacob's family, and thereby saved from certain death. But who are the *anti-chosen,* who oppose God and his chosen? That doesn't develop until later in the story when "there arose a new king over Egypt . . . [who] knew nothing about Yosef," pitting himself against the God of Israel and his chosen people, bringing judgment upon himself and Egypt as well (Exod 1:8).

Both the Joseph saga and the story of the Exodus refer to *a chosen place.* In the Joseph story, for a time, all of Egypt is *the chosen place* where *the chosen people* experience blessing. And even when Egypt becomes inhospitable due to oppression under Pharaoh and the ten plagues, God sets apart a *place of blessing* for his *chosen people.* Before the third plague comes upon Egypt we read, "I will set apart the land of Goshen, where my people live—no swarms of insects will be there—so that you can realize that I am Adonai, right here in the land . . . I will distinguish between my people and your people" (Exod 8:18–19, 22–23 in Christian Bibles). Goshen will later cease to be the place of blessing, as God sends Israel forth toward the land promised to their ancestors.

The pattern is clear and found frequently in the Tanak. There is a synergy between a *chosen person,* a *chosen people,* a *chosen provision*—that blessing which God has ordained for his people—a *chosen place* where blessing is experienced, *the also-provided-for* who are blessed along with and because of *the chosen,* and, always somewhere, whether in the background or foreground, *the anti-chosen* who oppose God's purposes and his people. All of these types of *dramatis personae* and scene-setting form the context in which God enacts the drama of what Walter C. Kaiser, Jr. calls *the promise:* his blessing plan for Israel, the nations, and the cosmos, as defined in the various covenants interwoven in Scripture's stories.[8] This plan of blessing is the grand narrative.[9]

To grasp God's grand narrative, we must do more than understand the stereotypical roles played by his characters. We also need to understand something that links the stories together, and that something is *covenant.*

---

8   Walter C. Kaiser, Jr. is the quintessential promise theologian, having addressed this subject from every conceivable angle over a fruitful and brilliant writing and teaching career. This exploration, which has fascinated him and all those privileged to sit under his teaching, is in turn rooted in his fascination with an old book (Willis Judson Beecher, *The Prophets and the Promise: Being for Substance),* variously reprinted but now available in a 2002 reprint from Wipf and Stock. Although Kaiser views Beecher's writing on the prophets to be dated, he remains enamored of his writing on the promise. In addition to Kaiser's voluminous writings, the concept is also to be found partially in Paul and Elizabeth Achtemeir, *The Old Testament Roots of our Faith* (Abingdon Press, 1962), and more completely in George Bristow, *The Promise of God: God's Unchangeable Purpose Through Human History* (Grand Rapids, MI.: Gospel Folio Press, 1997). Kaiser states, "Promise theology would suggest that there is a built-in category [the promise] announced by revelation in the text and explicitly understood by all the writers of Scripture to be the unifying theme in both testaments incorporating the inclusiveness of a 'corporate solidarity' of all the people named, yet one which can be so sharpened in focus that this corporateness yields up the unique individual who epitomizes the whole group and its calling. Herein lies a divinely revealed solution to the continuity problem. Nevertheless, subsumed under one eternal promise are the aspects of discontinuity and variety which are inherent in the promise itself from the beginning and explicitly declared to be elements of discontinuity by the Biblical writers." ["The Eschatological Hermeneutics of Evangelicalism: Promise Theology." *JETS 13* (1970) 92–96] 93.

9   In all of his writings, Kaiser is quite specific as to the nature and details of this promise plan of blessing, while others, equally enthralled with God's master plan, see aspects that Kaiser does not highlight. One example is R. Kendall Soulen who sees woven throughout the warp and woof of Scripture the principle of complementarity, of which he says, "God's work as Consummator engages the human family in a historically decisive way in God's election of Israel as a blessing to the nations. The resulting distinction and mutual dependence of Israel and the nations is the fundamental form of the economy of consummation through which God initiates, sustains, and ultimately fulfills the one human family's destiny for life with God. So conceived, God's economy of consummation is essentially constituted as an economy of mutual blessing between those who are and who remain different" [R. Kendall Soulen, *The God of Israel and Christian Theology.* Minneapolis:Augsburg/Fortress Press, 1996] 111.

Covenants: How God Moves His Great Narrative Forward

It is through covenants that God *defines, structures,* and *distributes* his provision for all we have named. Covenants link the stories together, and later stories refer back to them as a means of establishing continuity.

We use the term frequently, but coming up with a good definition of *covenant* isn't easy. A formal definition might be:

> *An elected, as opposed to natural, relationship of obligation established under divine sanction.*[10]

Or a less formal one:

> *A divinely structured relationship imposing obligations.*

This last one is quite helpful, because covenants always indicate obligations undertaken either by God, the Great King, or by his servants, or by both.

While earlier authorities spoke of covenants as either *conditional* or *unconditional*, more recently scholars have taken instead to speaking of the following two categories:

---

10   G. P. Hugenberger. *Marriage as Covenant: A Study of Biblical Law and Ethics Governing Marriage, Developed from the Perspective of Malachi.* In *Vetus Testamentum Supplement, 52;* Leiden: E.J. Brill. 1994, 171. For a fine and authoritative exploration of scholarly discussion on the definition of "covenant" see Scott Hahn, "Covenant in the Old and New Testaments: Some Current Research (1994–2004)." *Currents in Biblical Research 3.2* (2005) 263–292, also his *Kinship by Covenant: A Canonical Approach to the Fulfillment of God's Saving Promises.* The Anchor Yale Bible Reference Library. New Haven: Yale University Press, 2009. See also D.J. McCarthy, "Covenant in the Old Testament," *Catholic Biblical Quarterly 27* (1965) 217–240. For the distinctions between grant covenants and suzerain-vassal treaties, see, Moshe Weinfeld, "The Covenant of Grant in the Old Testament and in the Ancient Near East." *JAOS 90.2* (1970) 184–203, and "Covenant Terminology." *JAOS 93.2* (1973) 182–196. Definitions for "covenant" will vary according to the sources consulted and their perspectives on the related issues. A seminal source relating biblical covenants to precedents in collateral cultures is G.E. Mendenhall, "Covenant Forms in Israelite Tradition." *Biblical Archaeology 17* (1956) 50–76.

Grants: in which God, the Great King, obligates himself to provide benefits/blessings to his servants in recognition of their faithfulness to him.

Treaties: Also called *suzerain-vassal treaties,* in which God, the Great King, in consideration of blessings already bestowed upon an individual or a people (the vassal), stipulates what the vassal must do to honor him and thereby continue experiencing the benefits of relationship with him rather than earning his censure.

Looking at some well-known Bible stories of the establishing of covenants helps us appreciate the distinction between grants and treaties. All of this will help us better appreciate the Son of David and his crucial role in bringing these covenants to their fullest expression.

God's Covenant with Abraham

God's covenant with Abraham and his descendants is a *grant,* not dependent upon the reciprocity of the recipient.[11] All other blessing for Israel and the nations depends upon this foundational covenant. Walter Kaiser sees it as forming the foundation of a trilogy of covenants so closely related that he terms them the *Abrahamic-Davidic-New Covenant.*[12]

Depending upon how thinly the categories are sliced, various authorities differ in their breakdown of the blessings provided by the Abrahamic Covenant. Since the Bible does not name these categories, each scholar chooses whatever

11 The main passages where this covenant is developed are Gen 12:1–3; 13:14–17; 15:2–21; 17:1–21; 22:15–18; confirmed to Isaac in 26:3–5, 24; and to Jacob, 28:13–15; 35:9–12; and 46:1–4. Because it is so foundational to the entire Bible, it is neither possible nor wise to attempt to list every biblical passage alluding to this covenant: the data is far too extensive for that.

12 Walter C. Kaiser, Jr. "The Blessing of David: The Charter for Humanity." In *The Law and the Prophets: Oswald T. Allis Festschrift,* edited by John Skilton, 298–318. Philadelphia: Presbyterian and Reformed, 1974, 298. We will be examining these three covenants first, and covering the equally crucial Sinai/ Mosaic Covenant later.

labels he/she prefers. The following list of categories of covenantal blessing is typical and can be easily aligned with the features we earlier noted to be interwoven in Scripture's narratives:

- God would make Abraham a great nation (the chosen people)
- He would bless him (*the chosen person*)
- He would make his name great (*the chosen person*)
- Abraham and his seed would be a blessing to others (*the also-provided-for*)
- God would bless those who blessed him (*the also-provided-for*)
- God would curse those who cursed him (*the anti-chosen*)
- God would give to him innumerable descendants (*the chosen people*)
- Through Abraham and his seed God would distribute his blessing to all the peoples/families/nations of the earth (*the also-provided-for*)
- God would give to Abraham's seed the land he entered after leaving his homeland (*the chosen place*)

God's covenantal purpose, his blessing plan, his promise for Israel, the nations, and the cosmos, advances steadily throughout the Tanak—taking a giant leap forward in the story of David, King of Israel, with whom God also makes a covenant.

God's Covenant with David

The story is a familiar one. David has risen to the throne of Israel and is living in a palace, while the divine throne, the Ark of God, is sitting in a tent. Speaking to the Prophet Nathan, David comments on the incongruity of it all. Nathan encourages him to proceed as he intends—to build a temple for the God of Israel. That night, God corrects Nathan in a dream, who returns to David, with a message from the Holy One that echoes notes struck in the covenant with Abraham:

"I will make for you a great name" (2 Sam 7:9, RSV).

"I will appoint a place for my people Israel, and will plant them, that they may dwell in their own place, and be disturbed no more . . . and I will give you rest from all your enemies" (2 Sam 7:10–11, RSV).

These statements echo God's covenantal words to Abraham, Isaac, and Jacob that Abraham's name would be great, and those who curse him will be cursed, that they would possess the gates of their enemies, and of course, that God would bring his people to a place where they would be blessed.

In this case, David, rather than Abraham, is the chosen person, and the text goes on to speak of God extending this blessing to his chosen recipients in three ways: *a close-at-hand descendant, a chain of Davidic kings,* and *an ultimate Davidic king.*

First, covenant blessing through *a close-at-hand descendant* who shall come forth from his body, who would build a house for God's name, whom we know to be Solomon.[13]

Second, because his throne will be established forever, and neither David nor Solomon lived forever, God promises *a chain of Davidic kings* with whom God would share great power and intimacy.[14] They would be called sons of God, and God would be called their father.[15] If any individual in the kingly line sinned he would "punish him with a rod

---

13   2 Sam 7:12–13. Solomon foreshadows Yeshua the Messiah who will also build a house for God's Name (Matt 16:18; 1 Pet 2:4–10).

14   2 Sam 7:16.

15   2 Sam 7:14; see also Psa 2:7.

and blows," without this lapse extinguishing the promise God is making to the line of David that "your house and your kingdom will be made secure forever before you; your throne will be set up forever" (2 Sam 7:14, 16).

Third, as the prophets make clear, God would raise up *an ultimate descendant of David,* the Messiah, who would indeed reign forever.[16] He would be the ultimate chosen person through whom the chosen people would be blessed, and with them, all nations, families, and peoples of the world.[17]

Relating the Abrahamic and Davidic Covenants to the New Covenant in Tanak

Some think that the benefits delivered through the New Covenant are qualitatively superior to any *earthly, material* benefits, such as those we have mentioned, because they are fundamentally *spiritual.*[18] Although common, this viewpoint cannot withstand close scrutiny. A close inspection of New Covenant promises reveals that the Abrahamic, Davidic, and New Covenants are strongly related, that the New Covenant carries the earlier ones to completion, and that the New Covenant is equally concerned with *physical and political* dimensions, not merely *spiritual and redemptive ones:*[19]

- Regathering of the Israelites (Jer 32:37–40; Ezek 36:24, 28, 33; 37:21)

---

16 Cf. 1 Chron 17:14; Isa 9:7; Psa 45:6; 72:5, 17; 89:36–37; Luke 1:32–33; Heb 1:8; Rev 11:15.

17 In the Apostolic Witness we read of how, through the Messiah, a new category is forged as a way is opened whereby other nations of the world may become "the also chosen" or "the newly chosen." Such do not become Jews, but they do become part of the commonwealth of Israel (Eph 2), fully part of the people of God.

18 The division between physical/political and redemptive/spiritual concerns is artificial, being not so much related to the text as to post-Platonic philosophical categories.

19 This listing taken from Michael A. Grisanti, "The Davidic Covenant." *The Master's Seminary Journal, 10:2* (Fall 1999:233–250), 249, fn. 68.

- Repossession of the Land of Promise (Jer 24:6; 31:28; 32:41; Amos 9:15)

- Taming of the animal kingdom (Ezek 34:25–27; cf. Isa 11:6–9)

- Agricultural prosperity (Ezek 34:25–27; 36:30, 34–36; Amos 9:13)

- Cessation of war and the reign of peace (Jer 30:10; Ezek 24:28; 36:6, 15; 39:26)

- Reuniting Israel in one kingdom (Jer 50:4; Ezek 34:23; 37:22)

- Israel ruled by one king (Ezek 34:23; 37:22, 24)

- A sanctuary rebuilt in Jerusalem (Ezek 37:26–27a)

The New Testament/Covenant ratified in Yeshua's life, death, and resurrection does not one-up the covenants with Abraham and with David through being in some manner qualitatively superior. Rather it ratifies these covenants by bringing them to their *predestined consummation.*

Relating the Abrahamic and Davidic Covenants to the New Covenant in the Apostolic Witness[20]

Are there texts in the Apostolic Witness that connect the Abrahamic and Davidic covenants to the New Covenant promised by Jeremiah 31 and Ezekiel 36—37? Actually there are many such texts, and once you begin finding them, they seem to crop up everywhere.

For example, Luke's Gospel and the Book of Acts repeatedly make explicit the connections between the New Covenant established through Yeshua and the Abrahamic and Davidic covenants. The angel Gabriel tells Miriam, the mother of Yeshua, that her holy child will inherit the throne

---

20   In this essay, the term *Apostolic Witness* is used for that set of documents more commonly called the New Testament.

of his father David, thus situating the birth of Messiah squarely in the Davidic covenant.

In Miriam's song, the Magnificat, we read of how, in Yeshua, God is coming to the aid of Israel in remembrance of his mercy to "our fathers" (the patriarchs) as a demonstration of God's faithfulness "to Avraham and his seed forever" (Luke 1:55). Says Bible scholar Craig Blaising:

> Mary's song reveals her belief that the one whom she would bear to fulfill the promises to David would also fulfill the promises made to Abraham. In her mind the fulfillment of the Davidic covenant was the means by which the Abrahamic promise would be accomplished.[21]

Earlier in Luke, Zechariah prophesies concerning his son John, "Praised be Adonai, the God of Israel, because he has visited and made a ransom to liberate his people by raising up for us a mighty Deliverer who is a descendant of his servant David . . . that he might show the mercy promised to our fathers—that he would remember his holy covenant, the oath he swore before Avraham avinu" (Luke 1:68–73).[22] Again, the events of the Apostolic Witness, pointing to the *New Covenant*—accomplished in and through Yeshua—are seamlessly related to the *Abrahamic* and *Davidic covenants*. Walter Kaiser is right to relate these three together as a bonded unity.

Once one begins to look for it, one cannot avoid seeing how richly apostolic preaching harmoniously relates these three covenants together. As but one example among many, in Acts 3:12–26, Peter portrays Yeshua as the servant of the God of Abraham, Isaac, and Jacob, who brings Israel

---

21 Craig Blaising, "The Fulfillment of the Biblical Covenants." In *Progressive Dispensationalism*, edited by Craig A. Blaising and Darrell Bock, 174–211. Grand Rapids: Bridgepoint Books, 2000, 187–188.

22 Note as well how the reference to God raising up a horn of salvation evokes Davidic covenantal texts from the Older Testament: Ps 89:17, 24; 132:17; 2 Sam 7:12.

back to him (invoking Isa 49:5–6, one of the Servant Songs naming the Messiah as God's servant). Peter declares him to be the mediator of the blessings promised in the Abrahamic covenant, involving blessing for the nations (*the also-provided-for*) and for Israel, through bringing her to repentance. Peter takes an *already/not yet* perspective, looking forward to the culmination of that covenant in the future (with its *national* and *territorial* blessings). Again, Craig Blaising notes the connections:

> Peter's sermon confirms that blessings of the Abrahamic covenant are mediated by the Christ. As the Davidic covenant is fulfilled with Him, so the blessings of the Abrahamic covenant are fulfilled with respect to its various recipients. . . . Certain blessings are now available. Other blessings await the time of His return.[23]

We find the same connections in Paul's messages in Acts. Yeshua is a *descendant of David* (Acts 13:23; cf. 2 Sam 7:12). Paul spoke of a promise to the fathers now brought to pass for the children by which he means promises made to David and his descendants now come to pass in Yeshua (Acts 13:32–33). His reference to Yeshua being the Son of God is also clearly Davidic covenantal language:

> This raising up of Jesus son of David from the dead, His title *Son of God,* His enthronement at the right hand of God, and his activity of blessing Jews and all other people who bless Him, who trust in Him, are all aspects of the Davidic promise.[24]

A full listing of allusions connecting the New Covenant established by Yeshua with the Abrahamic and Davidic covenants is far too extensive to be covered fully here. But perhaps this quotation from a prominent theologian will

---

23 Blaising, "The Fulfillment of the Biblical Covenants," 189.
24 Blaising, 177–178, emphasis in the original.

underscore how strong and central this theme is in the preaching of the apostles:

The teaching in Luke and Acts that the Christ, the anointed king, is the one who mediates the blessings of the Abrahamic covenant agrees completely with . . . the Davidic covenant in the Old Testament, especially Psalm 72. Furthermore, this Old Testament background helps to interpret Paul's remarks in Galatians 3 about Christ fulfilling the promises to Abraham (Galatians 3:16–29). . . . Paul appears to be arguing that the Davidic covenant has structured the seed of Abraham in such a way that the blessing of the covenant first of all envisions the King, a single individual, and then through him all the other recipients.[25]

This concurs with what we have already seen concerning how God blesses a *chosen person,* and through him a *chosen people* and the *also-provided-for.*

Yeshua and the New Covenant Prophesied by Jeremiah

When, at the Last Supper, Yeshua relates his coming death to the forgiveness of sins and mentions "the New Covenant, ratified by my blood" (Lk 22:20), or "the New Covenant, my blood shed on behalf of many, so that they may have their sins forgiven" (Matt 26:28). This echoes the language and concerns of the New Covenant passage in Jeremiah 31:31–34. Paul himself echoes Yeshua's language when reporting on Yeshua's institution of this rite (see 1 Cor 11:25–29; 10:16).

Paul and the New Covenant Prophesied by Jeremiah and Ezekiel

The New Covenant prophesied in the Tanak is clearly referenced in the Apostolic Witness when Paul identifies

---

25   Blaising, 189–190.

himself and his coworkers as "workers serving a new covenant" (2 Cor 3:6), echoing aspects of New Covenantal language from the Tanak. His language and themes are clearly evocative of the Jeremiah 31 and Ezekiel 36—37 contexts.

Pauline Language	Prophetic Language
You are a letter from the Messiah placed in our care, *written not with ink but by the Spirit* of the living God, not on stone tablets but on human hearts (2 Cor 3:3).	"This is the covenant I will make with the house of Israel after those days," says Adonai: "I will put *my Torah within them and write it on their hearts"* (Jer 31:32).
He has even made us competent to be workers serving a New Covenant, the essence of which is *not a written text but the Spirit.* For the written text brings death, but *the Spirit gives life* (2 Cor 3:6).	I will put *my Spirit inside you and cause you to live by my [written] laws,* respect my rulings and obey them . . . I will put *my Spirit in you; and you will be alive* (Ezek 36:27; 37:14).

What all of this means is that the Apostolic Witness portrays the New Covenant from Jeremiah and Ezekiel as being established in the death of Yeshua. At least a foretaste of its promised blessings are now being granted to Jews and Gentiles who are believers in him, while other features promised in that covenant are seen as delayed until Messiah returns, including the national and territorial promises in Jeremiah 31:31, 36 and Ezekiel 36:28 and 37:14.

Forgiveness of Sins: A Central Aspect for Jeremiah, Ezekiel, and the Apostolic Witness

Forgiveness of sins is another core aspect of the New Covenant prophesied by Jeremiah and Ezekiel (Jer 31:34; Ezek 36:33; 37:23). It is therefore striking to see how central the message of *forgiveness of sins* is in the proclamation of Yeshua's identity and mission. We see this theme of forgiveness in Yeshua's commissioning of his disciples (Luke 24:47) and in the preaching of the apostles faithfully following from Yeshua's commissioning.

Peter in Acts 2:38 urges his audience to "turn from sin, return to God, and each of you be immersed on the authority of Yeshua the Messiah into forgiveness of your sins." Paul in Acts 13:38–39 rejoices that "through this man is proclaimed forgiveness of sins" and contrasts what Yeshua has done with Torah, of which he says his audience "could not be cleared by the Torah of Moshe" from transgressions.

This forgiveness of sins must be seen in the broader context of *the blessing or provision component* of the Abrahamic covenant, which had always had both Israel and the nations in view. Finally, it is clear that the apostolic gospel highlights this forgiveness theme from Jeremiah and Ezekiel. Paul even speaks of this message of forgiveness through Messiah's death as "among the first things I passed on to you" (1 Cor 15:3).

The Coming of the Spirit: A Prophesied New Covenant Blessing

Another theme in the prophetic promises of the New Covenant concerns the Spirit of God. God's Spirit renews his people and empowers aspects of knowledge, love, and ethical-religious renewal. Paul's language in 2 Corinthians 3:6–18 is strongly reminiscent of Ezekiel 36—37.

Pauline Language in 2 Corinthians 3—4 about the New Covenant	Language in Ezekiel 36—37 about the New Covenant
"ministers of a new covenant" (3:6) "ministry of the Spirit" (3:8) "our inner nature is being renewed" (4:16)	"and a *new spirit* I will put within you" (36:26) "I will put *my Spirit* within you and cause you to walk in my statutes and be careful to observe my ordinances" (36:27) "And I will put *my Spirit* within you, and you shall live" (37:14)
"on tablets of human hearts" (3:3) "the Spirit gives life" (3:6) "a veil lies over their hearts" (3:15)	"A new heart I will give you, and a new spirit I will put within you" (36:26) "take out of your flesh the heart of stone" (36:26)
"will raise us also with Yeshua and bring us with you into his presence" (4:14) "an eternal weight of glory beyond all comparison" (4:17)	"My dwelling place will be with them; and I will be their God and they shall be my people" (37:27)

The Unity of Abrahamic, Davidic, and New Covenants and the Place of the Mosaic

All of this blessing is in the end rooted in the three-fold matrix of the Abrahamic, Davidic, and New Covenants. Despite the diversity of his dealings, underneath all is an underlying unity:

In his present and future Davidic ministry, Jesus receives and mediates the blessings of the Abrahamic Covenant. In Him and through Him that covenant is and will be fulfilled. His mediation of the blessing extends to al peoples, to Jews and Gentiles who trust in Him. But He mediates it in stages, with the national and political blessings awaiting the dispensation of His return.[26]

Nor should we omit the Mosaic Covenant in God's blessing plan for the nations, for it is a means by which the blessings promised the descendants of Abraham, Isaac, and Jacob are administered to their descendants. The following chart helps to underscore the kind of unity and diversity I have been highlighting.

---

26   Blaising, "The Fulfillment of the Biblical Covenants," 193–4.

Covenant	Chosen Person	Chosen People	Persons Also Provided for	Chosen Place	Chosen Provision (some key terms)
Abrahamic	Abraham, Isaac, Jacob, Joseph	Descendants of Jacob (Israel), Seed of Abraham/Jacob	All the nations, families, peoples of the earth	Promised Land	A great nation, a great name; blessing, innumerable seed, land of promise, bless those who bless you, curse those who curse you
Mosaic	Moses	Descendants of Jacob (Israel), Seed of Abraham/Jacob	Nations living at peace with Israel	Wilderness, ultimately, Promised Land	Blessings listed in Lv 26:4–12 show how promises of Ab Covenant are manifest in the Mosaic: productivity, peace, power, population, provision, presence
Davidic	David, Davidic Kings Messiah	Descendants of Jacob (Israel), Seed of Abraham/Jacob	Same	Promised Land and all the earth	A great name; descendants (seed); an appointed place where Israel would live in safety from their enemies; sonship; intimate relationship (my people)
Newer Covenant (OT Terms)	Chosen One, Servant, Messiah, The Branch, Son of David, the Root of Jesse, etc.	Descendants of Jacob (Israel), Seed of Abraham/Jacob	Same	Promised Land and all the earth	Regathering of the Israelites; repossession of the Land of Promise; taming of the animal kingdom; agricultural prosperity; cessation of war and the reign of peace; reuniting Israel in one kingdom; Israel ruled by one king; a sanctuary rebuilt in Jerusalem
Newer Covenant (NT Terms)	Messiah, Son of David, Root of David, Yeshua, Son of David, etc.	Those whom God has called, both from Israel and the nations	Same	Promised Land and all the earth; entire cosmos	Gentiles becoming the people of God; inheriting the earth as Israel inherits the Land of Israel

YESHUA'S DAVIDIC OFFICE: PRESENT OR FUTURE?[27]

Imprinted by classical dispensationalism, some will hold that Yeshua's office as the Son of David is nice, "but that's for later. " Some are convinced this Davidic office will only be actualized in a future millennial reign when the Messiah rules from Jerusalem. Yet there are many others who would instead argue that Scripture portrays Yeshua's reign as having already begun, even if it not yet fully manifested.[28] This is my position, and following are some reasons for it.

Peter's Verdict on the Present Reign of the Son of David

In his Day of Pentecost sermon, Peter refers to "this Yeshua [whom God raised up] . . . exalted to the right hand of God; [who] has received from the Father what he promised, namely, the Ruach Hakodesh . . . which you are both seeing and hearing" (Acts 2:32–33). This talk about being "raised up . . . exalted to the right hand of God" is enthronement language. Peter further argues from Psalm 16 that David himself predicted "that his descendant would be raised up from the dead incorruptible, and in this way,

---

27 Since this study is addressed to the Messianic Jewish community, I will be restricting my focus to the Son of David's office with respect to the Jewish people. This is not to deny his significance for the nations, as is attested in Isaiah 11:10; Amos 9:12 (cf. Acts 15:15–21); Micah 5:2–3. For an exposition of the interfacing of God's mission for the Messianic Jewish world and the church, see my *Christians and Jews Together*. Eugene, OR: Wipf and Stock, 2009, available from www.MJTI.com.

28 Kaiser is one of those scholars who hold that Yeshua's reign is "already" even if there are aspects of that reign that are "not yet." "There is a 'now-already' aspect of the kingdom's appearance, as well as a 'not yet' future part of that same kingdom. . . . Thus, while the King is not yet visible in his kingdom, the kingdom nevertheless has begun and is effectively and powerfully operating through Christ's disciples and his church." Walter C. Kaiser, Jr., *Recovering the Unity of the Bible: One Continuous Story, Plan, and Purpose*. Grand Rapids: Zondervan, 2009, 137. See also Darrell L. Bock, "The Reign of the Lord Jesus." In *Dispensationalism, Israel and the Church*, edited by Craig Blaising and Darrell L. Bock. Grand Rapids: Zondervan, 1992, 38.

He would be seated upon His throne."[29] Furthermore, in the same context, Peter references Psalm 110 speaking of David's Son exalted to God's right hand. He argues that this was fulfilled through Yeshua's resurrection, something that in apostolic preaching always connotes his ascension and seating at the Father's right hand as well. Peter drives his point home forcefully: "Let the whole house of Israel know beyond doubt that God has made him both Lord and Messiah this Yeshua, whom you executed on a stake" (Acts 2:36). Later, in his address to the Sanhedrin, he clearly alludes to Yeshua's current kingly office when he says, "God has exalted this man at his right hand as Ruler and Savior, in order to enable Israel to do *t'shuvah* [repent] and have her sins forgiven" (Acts 5:31). If Peter had wanted to communicate that Yeshua's reign as the Son of David lies dormant until some far off millennium, he certainly did a poor job making his point!

Paul's Verdict on the Present Reign of the Son of David

When preaching in Antioch of Pisidia, Paul connects the raising up spoken of in 2 Samuel 7:12, Psalm 16, and Isaiah 55:3, all Davidic Covenantal texts, with Yeshua's resurrection. For Paul

> . . . the raising up of Jesus Son of David from the dead, his title Son of God, His enthronement at the right hand of God, and His activity of blessing Jews and all other people who bless Him, who trust in Him, are all aspects of the Davidic promise. The New Testament repeatedly proclaims these as presently fulfilled.[30]

---

29   Ac 2:30–31. In *Progressive Dispensationalism*, edited by Craig A. Blaising and Darrell L. Bock. Grand Rapids: Baker Book House, 1993, 177, emphasis in the original.

30   Blaising and Bock, 177–8.

Even Paul's use of the term "Son of God" relates to Yeshua's identity as King Messiah, Son of David. In Romans 1:3–4, Paul uses the term "Son of God" in two distinct ways, in reference to his divine, eternal, essential sonship in verse three when he speaks of Yeshua as God's Son who is "descended from David physically," thus implying that his intrinsic sonship was prior to his incarnation, that indeed, he was the Son of God in a certain sense before he ever became the Son of David. But Paul goes on to speak in verse 4 of Yeshua being "demonstrated to be Son of God spiritually, set apart by his having been resurrected from the dead; he is Yeshua the Messiah, our Lord." In this phrase, Paul speaks of Yeshua's kingly sonship as the Davidic King. All of Israel's kings were called God's Son, a striking term of intimacy. David McLeod brings this point home for us:

> Verse 4 must be read in light of Nathan's promise to David that God would adopt David's son as His own. David's son would [through being enthroned] become God's Son (Ps. 2:7, 12; Acts 2:36; 4:26–28; 5:31; 10:42; 13:33). . . . In verse 4 it (the term "Son") is used of his office. . . . At his resurrection, then, Jesus, the Son of David was "appointed" or "installed" or "enthroned" as God's [Messianic reigning Davidic] Son.[31]

---

31 David J. McCleod, "Eternal Son, Davidic Son, Messianic Son: An Exposition of Romans 1:1–7." *Bibliotheca Sacra 162* (January–March 2005:76–94) 86–88. To better understand the enthronement imagery used of Jesus the Son of David in the Acts and the Epistles, see McLeod's discussion of *horisthentos huiou theou,* commonly translated "declared the Son of God" (Rom 1:4) where he convincingly demonstrates that the verb *horidzo* more properly means "to appoint," "constitute," or "install," which is its meaning in all other New Testament uses (Luke 22:2; Acts 2:23; 10:42; 11:29; 17:26; Heb 4:7). "At his resurrection, then, Jesus is 'not just declared to be the Son of God: He was actually instituted the Son of God' in this messianic and Davidic sense" (Ibid., 88, internal quotes from Paul Beasley Murray, "Romans 1:3f: An Early Confession of Faith in the Lordship of Jesus." *Tyndale Bulletin 31* (1980: 147–54) 152–54.

There Is No Excuse for Not Serving the Son of David Now

Not even those who remain unconvinced, who insist that Yeshua is not yet exercising his Davidic kingly role, can justify a passive wait and see attitude concerning how to respond to his allegedly dormant office. This is because Scripture never announces future events as mere information, or simply to satisfy curiosity. Instead, future events are prophetically revealed to spur God's people to present action.

That this is the case is made clear in 2 Peter 3:9–14, which calls us to wholehearted retooling of our lives in view of the cataclysmic and apocalyptic end awaiting the present cosmic order:

> The Lord is not slow in keeping his promise, as some people think of slowness; on the contrary, he is patient with you; for it is not his purpose that anyone should be destroyed, but that everyone should turn from his sins. However, the Day of the Lord will come "like a thief." On that Day the heavens will disappear with a roar, the elements will melt and disintegrate, and the earth and everything in it will be burned up. Since everything is going to be destroyed like this, what kind of people should you be? You should lead holy and godly lives, as you wait for the Day of God and work to hasten its coming. That Day will bring on the destruction of the heavens by fire, and the elements will melt from the heat; but we, following along with his promise, wait for new heavens and a new earth, in which righteousness will be at home. Therefore, dear friends, as you look for these things, do everything you can to be found by him without spot or defect and at peace.

The text calls for us to hasten the coming of the end through attentiveness and activism. Surely, this is the antithesis of passivity! And if the coming end of the cosmos calls for attentiveness and activism, how much more should we be alert and vigorous in hastening and looking forward to the coming of the Son of David who will rule and reign from Jerusalem? By what stretch of the imagination could anyone suppose the approaching footsteps of Messiah warrant nothing beyond doctrinal agreement? On the contrary, the approach of the Son of David calls for alertness and action of the highest order. Clearly we have work to do. But what kind of work will that be?

SIX STEPS TOWARD RIGHTLY SERVING THE SON OF DAVID NOW

To understand and undertake that work we must take at least six giant steps, difficult and demanding.[32] Perhaps what makes these steps hardest is that they involve repudiating and correcting past neglect. Yet, if the Messianic Jewish Congregational Movement is to experience and spark renewal, we must bite the bullet and begin.

Step One: We Must Restore Yeshua the Son of David to His Context

Ever since the Day of Pentecost, Yeshua, the risen and enthroned Son of David, has been advancing an agenda for Israel that must become our agenda too. This agenda, nicely summarized for us by Ezekiel (37:21–28), names seven aspects of God's end-time agenda for the Jewish people.[33] The following illustration highlights Yeshua, the Son of

---

32 None should read any sort of prioritization into the ordering of these steps, which are numbered for convenience rather than to suggest either sequence or relative importance.

33 This might be called "The Ezekiel Agenda," and I have called it, "The New Messianic Jewish Agenda." However, it could just as easily be called the Son of David's Agenda.

David, within this broader context of prophesied divine intentions for Israel and the nations.[34]

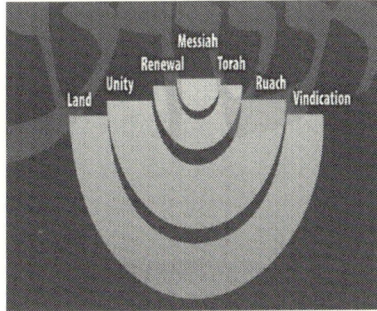

In this passage (37:21–28), Ezekiel reminds us that through the risen Messiah:

1. God will regather the Jewish people to the land he gave us forever.

2. God will unify us as a people.

3. God will bring the Jewish people to repentance-renewal.

4. God will gather us in allegiance to the Messiah.

5. God will cause the Jewish people to live in covenant faithfulness to the statutes and ordinances God has given to our ancestors.

6. God will cause us to communally experience the fullness of the Divine Presence.

7. By doing these things, God will vindicate his name in the sight of the nations.

Keeping these agenda points in mind, we will notice how these seven aspects of what could be called "The Son of

---

34   This illustration courtesy of Molly Hurley, of Teknigrammaton Graphics, http://www.teknigram.com/

David's Agenda" are underscored in events and teachings recorded in the Apostolic Witness. Consider for example Peter's first two sermons, recorded in Acts 2 and 3. On the Day of Pentecost, Peter highlights how the risen Son of David has sent forth the Spirit and his manifestations "which you are both seeing and hearing" (Acts 2:33). This sending of the Spirit refers to the third and sixth items mentioned by Ezekiel: bringing the Jewish people to repentance-renewal and causing us to communally experience the fullness of the Divine Presence. Peter's statement later, that God exalted Yeshua at his right hand to give repentance to Israel and forgiveness of sins, when read in the context of Ezekiel 37, also relates to the repentance-renewal of Israel. And certainly, Peter's call to Israel to "repent and turn to God, so that your sins may be erased; so that times of refreshing may come from the Lord's presence, and he may send the Messiah appointed in advance for you . . . as God said long ago, when he spoke through the holy prophets." (Acts 3:19–21) is pointing toward the outcomes prophesied in Ezekiel 36 and 37, summarized for us in the seven steps of the Son of David's Agenda.

The following chart makes clearer some of the parallels between Acts 2 and 3 and Ezekiel 36 and 37:

Ezekiel Says in 37:21–28	Peter Says (in Acts 2—3)
God will regather the Jewish people to the land he gave us forever.	"the time comes for restoring everything, as God said long ago, when he spoke through the holy prophets" (3:21); Surely this includes the multitudinous promises about the Land.
God will unify us as a people.	"Let the whole *house of Israel* know beyond doubt that God has made him both Lord and Messiah this Yeshua" (2:36); "Turn from sin, return to God, and each of you be immersed on the authority of Yeshua the Messiah into forgiveness of your sins, and you will receive the gift of the Ruach Hakodesh" (2:38).
God will bring the Jewish people to repentance-renewal.	"Turn from sin, return to God, and each of you be immersed on the authority of Yeshua the Messiah into forgiveness of your sins, and you will receive the gift of the Ruach Hakodesh" (2:38).
God will gather us in allegiance to the Messiah.	"Turn from sin, return to God, and each of you be immersed on the authority of Yeshua the Messiah into forgiveness of your sins" (2:38).
God will cause the Jewish people to live in covenant faithfulness to the statutes and ordinances God has given to our ancestors.	"You are the sons of the prophets; and you are included in the covenant which God made with our fathers . . . God has sent his servant whom he has raised up, so that he might bless you by turning each one of you from your evil ways" (3:25–26).
God will cause us to communally experience the fullness of the Divine Presence.	The events of Penetecost fulfill the prophecies of Joel about the outpouring of the Spirit (2:16–210); Yeshua, who received the promise of the Spirit, has poured out this which you see and here (2:33); Repent *every one of you* and be baptized and you shall receive the gift of the Holy Spirit (2:58).
By doing these things, God will vindicate his name in the sight of the nations.	"the time comes for restoring everything, as God said long ago, when he spoke through the holy prophets" (3:21); "You are the sons of the prophets; and you are included in the covenant which God made with our fathers... God has sent his servant whom he has raised up, so that he might bless you by turning each one of you from your evil ways" (3:25–26).

Richard Longenecker confirms the connection between Ezekiel 36—37 and these texts in the Apostolic Witness in his commentary on the Acts of the Apostles where he points out the clear connection between the renewal at Pentecost and the prophecies of restoration in Ezekiel 37, the focus of our considerations here, and the New Messianic Jewish/Son of David's Agenda.

> Ezekiel had prophesied of the wind as the breath of God blowing over the dry bones in the valley of his vision and filling them with new life (Ezek 37:9–114), and it was this wind of God's Spirit that Judaism looked forward to as ushering in the final Messianic Age. Thus Luke tells us that as a sign of the Spirit's coming on the early [Jewish] followers of Jesus, there was 'a sound like the blowing of a violent wind.'
>
> Judaism . . . expected that with the coming the of the Messianic Age there would be a special outpouring of God's Spirit, in fulfillment of Ezekiel 37, and that prophecy would once again flourish. And this is exactly what Luke portrays as having taken place at Pentecost among the followers of Jesus.[35]

Step Two: We Must Get Busy and Keep Busy Advancing the Son of David's Agenda

Yeshua told us to keep busy until his return. But there is a difference between keeping busy and doing busywork. Doing busy work is a waste of time, and keeping busy is an investment for eternity. How should we invest our resources of time, substance, and personnel in view of the approaching return of the Son of David? Surely, a major portion of the answer to this question is found in the Son of David's Agenda (the New Messianic Agenda, see above). As individuals,

---

35   Richard N. Longenecker, "The Acts of the Apostles." In *The Expositor's Bible Commentary, Vol. 9*, edited by F. E. Gaebelein. Grand Rapids, MI: Zondervan, 1981, 66–67. I am grateful to Michael Rydelnik for calling my attention to Longenecker's referencing Ezekiel 37 in connection with Acts 2.

congregations, and as a movement we must devote ourselves to advancing each item of this agenda as priority one commitments. Examples follow:

- God is bringing our people back to the Land at this time, so we should be demonstrating our commitment to aliyah by doing so ourselves, and by assisting and encouraging others who do so. This also would include providing financial support of various kinds, and support of legislation to expedite the enfolding of Messianic Jews in Israeli society.

- God is bringing the Jewish people to unity, so we must always remember and live out this principle: "the Jewish people are 'us,' not 'them.'"[36] Even in contexts where other Jews might seek to exclude us and discount us for our Yeshua faith, we must never be confused about our solidarity with them. We must continue to contribute to Jewish institutions, support Jewish causes, and labor for the wellbeing of all Jews everywhere.

- God is bringing the Jewish people to repentance-renewal, so we must assist and applaud all signs of a Jewish return to covenant faithfulness and joyful Torah living. Wherever this is happening, even where Yeshua is not yet named as Messiah and Lord, we should rejoice and provide support.

- God is bringing the Jewish people to allegiance to the Messiah, so we must unashamedly be his ambassadors to our people, recruiting other Jews to his service within the context of the Son of David's/ New Messianic Jewish Agenda. This is normally called "outreach," although one may argue that since it is an intra-communal affair, it is "inreach." Whatever the term, bringing our people to honor and serve

36 This is the fourth core value or core principle of Hashivenu, a Messianic Jewish think-tank. See http://hashivenu.org/index.php?option=com_content&view=art icle&id=47:principles&catid=35:principles&Itemid=54

Yeshua the Son of David by all legitimate means is an inescapable imperative.

- God is bringing the Jewish people back to covenant faithfulness, to renewed Torah living. We should be growing in our understanding of Torah and what obedience to Torah should look like for Messianic Jews. This means supporting and strengthening organizations like the Messianic Jewish Rabbinical Council, which seeks to promote Torah living among Messianic Jews. We should be applauding and assisting a return to Torah for all Jews everywhere. While it is true that many Jews are indifferent to Torah, we should be anything but indifferent. Calling Jews back to Torah is inextricably part of the message of repentance and faith we are commissioned to proclaim. The time is coming when it will be difficult to find any Jews indifferent to Torah, for the prophets wrote that God would write the Torah on our hearts, and through his Spirit and by his Messiah cause us to return to covenant faithfulness. We should be ahead of the curve, not behind it!

- God is bringing the Jewish people to a communal experience of the Divine Presence manifest in our midst. Therefore, we Messianic Jews should be praying with great fervor the words of the seventeenth blessing of the daily Amidah which ends, *"Baruch atah Adonai, hamachazir sh'khinato l'Tzion*—Blessed are you, Hashem, who restores the Divine Presence to Zion."* We should be prayerfully seeking the Divine Presence, and by living lives of obedience and love throw out the welcome mat to the Holy One, seeking the manifestation of his Presence in our midst. We should learn to discern and welcome signs of the Divine Presence being among us, teaching on these matters with combined bold expectation and wariness of manipulation.

- God is moving all history to that time when, through
his manifest power and mercy, he will vindicate
himself as Israel's God, and Israel as his people, a time
when Yeshua will be vindicated as his Son. Therefore,
we should be engaged in standing up for the Jewish
people, and for the honor of God and his Messiah
wherever these are challenged or brought under attack.
We are to be partisans for the honor of the God of Israel
and the Israel of God.

Step Three: We Must Reframe Our Thinking and Doing Around Jewish Covenantal Identity

In our thinking, feeling, and doing we must restore the
Jewish people to their identity as a people called by God
to glorify him in the context of communal Torah living.
Because this facet of the testimony of Scripture has been
neglected and undermined for centuries, it is imperative
that we reconfigure our thinking in this area.

Many in the Messianic Jewish Congregational Movement
as well as in the Jewish Missions Movement neglect or
discard the covenantal identity and responsibilities of the
Jewish people. This is due to prior, and to some degree,
subconscious ecclesial alliances, theological commitments,
and even financial entanglements.[37]

We have all distanced ourselves from *supersessionism.*
This is the view that *the church is the new Israel that has
forever superseded national Israel as the people of God.* The
result is that the church has become the sole inheritor
of God's covenant blessings originally promised to

---

37 Of our sibling relatives the Jewish missions, which Jewish mission would risk
alienating its support base by preaching that Jews who believe in Jesus should
obey Torah? What Jewish mission agency is not committed to a theology
that declares such Torah obedience to be no longer mandated, with a mailing
list sharing the same commitments? Missions are not alone in their need to
demonstrate fealty to people holding paradigms in some ways at variance with
an appropriate Messianic Jewish communal reality.

national Israel in the Old Testament.[38] Yet, although both the Messianic Jewish Congregational Movement and the Jewish Missions Movement have repudiated supersessionism, many in our movement are steeped in what I term *cryptosupersessionsm*. This involves *emptying Israel's chosenness of its meaning and weight through vacating her former distinctives*. Read on to see how this is deeply true in the area of our relationship to Torah.

Step Four: We Must Reframe Our Thinking About Torah and the Law of Messiah

Cryptosupersessionism exists wherever there is an unconscious and entrenched cluster of presuppositions assuming the expiration or setting aside of identity markers that formerly applied to the Jewish people, effectively nullifying Israel's covenantal uniqueness in whole or in part. Cryptosupersessionism is the more powerful because it is unconscious. In our ranks it is often those who speak loudest about the Jewish people and their chosenness who embrace cryptosupersessionist theological commitments vitiating Jewishness of its substance.

Consider the teaching, widely represented in our circles, that with the coming of Messiah/the New Covenant, the *Law of Moses* is categorically rendered inoperative, and that the only Law that applies to Jewish Yeshua-believers is the *Law of Christ*.[39]

---

38   Michael J. Vlach, "Defining Supersessionism." n.p. (cited 8 December 2008). Online: http://www.theologicalstudies.citymax.com/articles/article/1546226/17515.htm.

39   Confidence and consensus is waning concerning the commonly held assumption that the Law of Christ is to be defined as the commandments promulgated by Yeshua and the Apostles. Todd A. Wilson comments, "While the phrase [the Law of Christ] has traditionally been harmonized with Paul's negative portrayal of the law by treating the phrase either as a circumlocution for Christian living or as a reference to some other "law," a growing number of interpreters want to treat the "law of Christ" as a reference to the law of Moses." Wilson also surveys the widening group of exegetical opinion viewing

Since the Church too is subject only to the Law of Christ, is it not clear that this teaching involves nullifying a major identity marker that formerly differentiated the Jewish people from the other nations? Some protest that Jewish covenantal uniqueness is preserved through the Abrahamic Covenant instead of the Mosaic, but it is highly questionable that Jewish covenantal identity can be successfully transmitted inter-generationally on the basis of a mere recognition of ancient peoplehood, even if supported by a variety of seasonal celebrations.

When challenged on this point by a Jewish missionary who insisted the Abrahamic Covenant provided a sufficient foundation for such intergenerational identity transmission, I reminded him that he had just bragged to me about his son having read his *Haftarah* well at his recent *Bar Mitzvah*. I pointed out that this observance does not come out of the Abrahamic Covenant but out the fabric of Jewish Torah living. His own actions demonstrated how he needed more to sustain his son's Jewishness than reminders about the Abrahamic Covenant. Inevitably, jettisoning the *Law of Moses* and substituting the *Law of Christ* means reducing Jewishness to genetics and nostalgia, while assimilating Jews into a code of conduct and way of life indistinguishable from Gentile Christians—the same Law, the Law of Christ.

We in the Messianic Movement have declared *One Law Movements,* which postulate that Jews and Gentiles equally must keep the Law of Moses, to be seriously defective. Yet, whenever and wherever any in our ranks insist that Jews and Gentiles are only responsible to adhere to "the Law of Christ," this too is a One Law Movement, and equally defective.

Paul's "law of faith" and the "law of the Spirit of life" as referring likewise to the Law of Moses. See Todd A. Wilson, "The Law of Christ and the Law of Moses Reflections on a Recent Trend in Interpretation." *Current Issues in Biblical Research* (Volume 5.1:125–144). London, Thousand Oaks CA and New Delhi: SAGE Publications. Found online at http://cbi.sagepub.com/cgi/reprint/5/1/123.

Commenting on One Law Movements in a paper for the Union of Messianic Jewish Congregations, Russ Resnik and Dan Juster write:

> Paradoxically, One Law people undermine their own vision for "One People," by basing unity on a common response to Torah. In other words, they hope to achieve unity by producing unified Torah-based behavior among all believers. Scripture, however, portrays our unity as accomplished in Messiah himself.
>
> The letter to the Ephesians, which includes some of the strongest statements of unity within the body of believers, never posits the idea of One Law. Instead, it calls us to maintain "the unity of the Spirit in the bond of peace," for "there is one body and one Spirit, just as you were called in one hope of your calling; one Lord, one faith, one baptism; one God and Father of all, who is above all, and through all, and in you all" (4:4–6).
>
> The beauty of this God-given unity is that it honors and preserves biblical distinctions between diverse groups, particularly Jews and Gentiles.[40]

Their critique applies equally to the One Law of Christ/ Messiah perspective, which views both Jew and Gentile as obligated equally to the same body of law. The unity into which Messiah brings us is a *differentiated unity,* wherein Jews and Gentiles remain essentially different, distinct but not separate, and reconciled to one another despite their

---

40 Daniel Juster and Russ Resnik, "One Law Movements: A Challenge to the Messianic Jewish Community." Online: http://umjc.net/home-mainmenu-1/ faqs-mainmenu-58/14-umjc-faq/24-is-the-torah-only-for-jews.

Mark Kinzer is helpful here as well in his analysis of Markus Barth's treatment of the one new man of Ephesians 2:15 (Markus Barth, *Ephesians 1—3.* Garden City, NY: Doubleday, 1974). Barth defends his translation as reading "one new man consisting of two." See Mark S. Kinzer, *Postmissionary Messianic Judaism: Redefining Christian Engagement With the Jewish People.* Grand Rapids: Brazos Press, 2005, 167–171.

continuing distinctions. This is the marvelous *reconciling unity* that Messiah effects: *not uniformity,* lopping off distinctives; not some sort of enforced conformity, nor some utopian unanimity where all agree on every jot and tittle. In fact, the unity in Messiah of which Paul speaks is only represented where and when Messianic Jews live differently, in the context of Jewish covenantal life, and yet in unity with their Gentile brothers and sisters, who accept them in their differentness and who recognize that while such a lifestyle is not their own covenantal calling, they ought always to refrain from disparaging Jewish covenantal distinctives, or from casting aspersions on those who adhere to them. Unfortunately, covenantal Jewish living receives an ambivalent and sometimes hostile response even in Messianic Jewish congregational circles.

Advocating one Law of Christ/Messiah for Jew and Gentile alike consigns Jews to assimilation and, within two or three generations at most, communal extinction in almost every case. Although we all know exceptions, these are exceptions. The rule is assimilation and communal disintegration.[41] If we accept that Jewish Yeshua believers are subject to no religious law other than the same Law of Christ/Messiah to which the average white-bread Gentile in Tulsa, Oklahoma, subscribes, then we are fitting Jewish community and continuity into a plain pine box. It is time to say *Kaddish.*

One may further grasp the importance a Jewish return to Torah by considering what the Bible has to say about Jewish sin and the meaning of Jewish repentance.[42]

---

41 In a 1989 study, DellaPergola and Schmelz determined that absent conversion, no grandchildren of intermarriages continue to identify as Jews. Since intermarriage is so prevalent in our circles, when one factors in a disparagement of Jewish law-keeping, we must be honest and admit that we are greasing the skids toward assimilation and Jewish communal disintegration. Any other assessment seems dishonest and self-serving. See DellaPergola, S. and Schmelz, U.O. "Demographic Transformations of American Jewry: Marriage and Mixed Marriage in the 1980s." *Studies in Contemporary Jewry, Vol. 5.* (1989) 169–200.

42 For a convincing argument for the necessity of Torah adherence for Jewish

Step Five: We Must Reframe Our Thinking About Jewish Sin and Jewish Repentance

One would think that religious professionals who work among the Jewish people would have a clear idea of what it is that Jews must repent of, and what shape their repentance must take. Yet, as I travel and ask members of the Congregational and Missions Movements what it is for which Jews need to repent, and what shape that repentance must take, I am usually met with blank stares, and never with a uniform response. Behind those stares are people realizing that that they had never really thought about the question, perhaps because it seemed so obvious.

Sooner or later one will hear this answer: "Jewish people need to repent for their sins." But how do we know what those sins are for which Jews should repent? Are they just run of the mill standards of human decency that Jews, like others, stumble over from time to time, or, if you will, constantly?

Jewish sin is disobeying Torah. Kendall Soulen reminds us:

> Human sin is never merely the sin of the creature against the Creator-Consummator. Human sin is also always the sin of Jew and Gentile, of Israel and the nations.[43]

And in Romans 2:12, Paul indicates his agreement with this principle: "All who have sinned *without the law* will also perish *without the law,* and all who have sinned *under the law* will be judged *by the law*" (RSV). Who then is it that has sinned *under the law?* There can be only one answer to this question: the Jewish people. We Jews are a people born

---

communal continuity, see Elliott Abrams, *Faith or Fear: How Jews Can Survive in a Christian America.* New York: The Free Press, 1997.

43   R. Kendall Soulen, 153.

into a covenantal identity and responsibility to obey God's law. And the measure of our sin is our disobedience to this holy standard through a pattern of neglect or rebellion. If the measure of Jewish sin is disobedience to Torah, then Jewish repentance requires a return to Torah living. An honest assessment of Scripture calls for nothing less, as well as something more, for there is one more crucial aspect to Jewish sin and Jewish repentance.

Jewish sin is rejecting God's messengers. In both the Tanak and the Apostolic Witness these two measuring rods, Torah disobedience, and rejection of God's messengers, are found together.

One especially graphic passage is found in the Book of Nehemiah, written in the mid-5th century BCE. Chapters 8—10 describe the returning exiles renewing the covenant, and chapter 9 records a national historical retrospective and confession of sin. Reviewing the experience of the Israelites under Joshua, the text says, "Yet they disobeyed and rebelled against you, throwing your Torah behind their backs; they killed your prophets for warning them that they should return to you" (9:26). Notice that their disobedience is described as throwing God's Torah behind their backs, not wanting to hear it, not wanting to deal with it, not wanting to obey it. Notice as well how this is yoked to how they "killed your prophets for warning them that they should return to you." Here we have a description of Jewish sin (casting God's law behind our backs) and its linkage to killing the prophets/rejecting God's messenger who admonished us to return to God.

But what shape would that repentance take? Nehemiah provides an answer:

> You warned them, in order to bring them back to your Torah; yet they were arrogant. They paid no attention

to your mitzvot, but sinned against your rulings, which, if a person does them, he will have life through them. However, they stubbornly turned their shoulders, stiffened their necks and refused to hear (9:29).

The shape of Jewish turning back to God (repentance) is a return to Torah, to his commandments and ordinances, by which a person who does them shall live.[44] This text and others like it insist that Jewish sin is disobedience to Torah and rejection of his messengers, and Jewish repentance is acceptance of his messengers and a return to Torah living. But such answers are often rejected in the Messianic Jewish Congregational Movement and Jewish Missions Movement, due either to their inconvenience or to our adherence to other *cryptosupersessionistic* paradigms.

Some are sure to object that this is Old Testament revelation, no longer applicable after the coming of Messiah, itself an irksome argument. One of the best refutations of this objection is in Acts chapter 7, where we read of Stephen, the Hellenistic Jew and first martyr among the Jerusalem-based Yeshua believers. Here we see how he naturally portrays Jewish sin as a rejection of God's messengers, the prophets, and disobedience to Torah:

Stiffnecked people, with uncircumcised hearts and ears! You continually oppose the Ruach HaKodesh! You do the same things your fathers did! Which of the prophets did your fathers not persecute? They killed those who told in advance about the coming of the Tzaddik, and now you have become his betrayers and murderers!—you!—who receive the Torah as having been delivered by angels—but do not keep it! (Acts 7:51–53).

---

44 For a good understanding from a respected evangelical voice for law keeping as a way of life, as Jews know it to be, rather than as a way of death, as Christians are apt to see it, see Walter C. Kaiser, Jr., "Leviticus 18:5 and Paul: Do This and You Shall Live (Eternally?)." *JETS 14, No. 1* (Winter 1971) 19–28.

Notice carefully the two aspects of Jewish sin highlighted here: persecuting God's messengers, culminating in the betrayal and murder of the Messiah, and failing to keep Torah. These are directly parallel to the criteria outlined by Nehemiah, a pattern that occurs repeatedly in Scripture.[45]

Ezekiel's verdict on issues of Torah and Jewish renewal confirms this notion of Jewish sin. We have seen how Ezekiel 37:21–28 summarizes the Son of David's Agenda for Israel. Those who protest that this seems to be a bit of convenient proof-texting would do well to bear in mind how the structure of the entire Book of Ezekiel underscores this perspective and the coordinate roles of the Spirit of God and the Messiah in bringing Israel to repentance-renewal, and a return to covenant faithfulness in the context of Torah.

The Book of Ezekiel falls into four sections:

- Section One (Chapters 1—24) – judgments against Israel,

- Section Two (Chapter 25—32) – judgments against the nations,

- Section Three (Chapter 33:1–20) – a transitional passage echoing various motifs found in Section One in preparation for the next section.[46]

- Section Four (Ezekiel 3:21—48:35) – Israel's restoration.

Throughout the book one finds explicit and implicit echoes of Leviticus 18:5, "You are to observe my laws and

---

45 For other texts referring to the killing of the prophets/rejection of God's messengers, see 1 Kgs 18:4,13; 19:10; 2 Chr 24:20, 21; 36:16; Jer 26:20–23; Matt 21:21–43 (= Mark 12:1–12; Luke 20:9–19; Matt 23:33–46); Matt 23:34–39 (= Luke 13:31–35). For other texts referring to casting God's law behind our backs, see, for example, 1 Kgs 14:9, where the comparison is to casting God behind our backs, an even stronger metaphor for disobedience, and Ps 50:17, and texts too numerous to mention about disobedience to God's laws.

46 These include the watchman motif of 3:17–21 in Ezek 33:1–9, and the potential of life for the wicked man (representing Israel) originally found in 18:21–32.

rulings; if a person does them, he will have life through them," a key text in what is termed the "Holiness Code," itself a core section of priestly instruction in Leviticus.[47] This is not surprising considering that Ezekiel was a priest. The laws and rulings (or statutes and ordinances) are the *chukkim* and *mishpatim*, a common designation for God's commandments in Torah. Two emphases from Leviticus 18:5 weave throughout Ezekiel: the connection between keeping the statutes and ordinances of God (the *chukkim* and the *mishpatim*), and issues of life and death/ the blessing of being in the Land versus the curse of being in exile.[48]

Ezekiel scholar Preston Sprinkle indicates that the use of statutes and ordinances terminology in Leviticus is shorthand for obedience/disobedience to the covenant, and that Leviticus 18:5 refers not to specific legislations but to the entire revelation at Sinai![49] He demonstrates how Ezekiel clearly teaches that just as Israel's deterioration and exile, a

---

47 Leviticus 17—26 is a literary unit referred to as "the Holiness Code," due to its focus and characteristic vocabulary, especially the frequent use of the term kadosh (holy). Chapter 27 serves as a kind of appendix to the code. Chapter 26, the formal ending, chronicles the blessings attending Israel's covenant obedience and the curses consequent to her covenant disobedience, culminating in exile, a major preoccupation of the book of Ezekiel. This blessing or cursing is presented as contingent upon obedience or disobedience to the *chukkim/chukkot* and *mishpatim*, the statutes and judgments of Torah. This is made explicit in Lev 18:3, 5, 15, and especially verse 43, where the covenant disobedience that led to Israel's exile is directly equated with their violation of God's *chukkim* and *mishpatim*: "But the land shall be left by them, and enjoy its sabbaths while it lies desolate without them; and they shall make amends for their iniquity, because they spurned my ordinances (*mishpatai*), and their soul abhorred my statutes (*chukkotai*),"

48 Preston Sprinkle lists the following allusions to "walking in the statutes and ordinances" (Lev 18:5) in Ezekiel: 5:6–7, 11:12–20, 18:9,17, 19; cf. 21; 20:11, 13, 18, 19, 21; cf. 25; and 36:27, and 37:24, and reference to "life language" and the underlying verb, echoing the last clause in Lev 18:5, in 3:18, 21; 13:19, 22; 16:6; 18:9, 13, 17, 19, 21, 22, 23, 24, 27, 28, 32; and 20:11, 13, 21, 25. The verb then returns in 33:10–20, the transition section in vv. 20, 11, 12, 13, 15, 16, 19, and in the vision of the valley of dry bones in 37:1–14 ("Law and Life: Leviticus 18.5 in the Literary Framework of Ezekiel." *Journal for the Study of the Old Testament, Vol. 31.3* [2007, 275–293] 278).

49 Sprinkle, 281.

form of national death, was connected with her failure to walk in the statutes and judgments of Torah, so her national resurrection and renewal would necessitate a divinely engineered national return to obeying the very same statutes and judgments, the nuts and bolts of Torah living.

When the prophet speaks of Israel's restoration, we must not miss what he says in 36:27: "I will put my Spirit inside you and cause you to live by my laws, respect my rulings and obey them," which is "a divine response, or reversal, of the disobedience of Israel . . . fulfilled by Yahweh himself in his program of restoration."[50]

The Spirit of God intends and will accomplish Israel's return to covenant obedience (Torah living). Finally, Ezekiel teaches that this is also the goal of the Son of David: "My servant David will be king over them, and all of them will have one shepherd; they will live by my rulings and keep and observe my regulations" (37:24). Preston Sprinkle comments on this:

> Once again, it is Yahweh who radically reverses the situation by causing Israel to obey through the Davidic king. Since Israel was unable to 'do' the 'statutes and judgments,' Yahweh must incite obedience in the program of restoration.[51]

For Ezekiel, for the God of Israel, for the Spirit of God, for the Son of David, and for us as well, there can be no such thing as Jewish restoration and renewal apart from Jews returning to covenant obedience, the *mitzvot of Torah*. Anything less and anything else falls short of God's standards and intentions.

---

50 Sprinkle, 290.
51 Sprinkle, 291.

Step Six: We Must Reframe Our Thinking About Outreach/Evangelism to Mean Recruiting Our People to the Son of David's/New Messianic Jewish Agenda

Messianic Jewish outreach is not simply a matter of speaking to souls in flesh suits, of speaking of Messiah to people who just happen to be Jewish. No: true Messianic Jewish outreach requires us to reconnect with what it means that the person we are speaking to is a member of a covenant people whom we should be calling back to their identity and destiny through enlisting them in the service of the Son of David and his agenda.

Many reject this perspective, arguing that most Jews are secular. Granted! But if what we have been learning from Scripture is true, then part of our outreach responsibility to our fellow Jews involves calling them out of their secularity, back to Torah living, that way of life given to our ancestors as the means of communally honoring Him, and indeed a way of life to which we each and all remain covenantally obligated.[52]

In the late 1980s I heard a missionary to the Jews speaking at a meeting where he said:

> It is not our responsibility to look after Jewish continuity: God will take care of that. Our job is just to preach the gospel.

While some find this view commendable and "spiritual," I regard it to be a pious-sounding bundle of falsehood. That is why I spoke up at this meeting, challenging this missionary on the basis of what I term *the Mordecai Mandate,* derived from Mordecai's counsel to Esther.

---

52   In addition to the passages in Exod 19:8; 24:3, 7; Deut 5:27–28, which record and commend our ancestors agreeing to obey God's commandments, see Deut 29:10–15, which all commentators agree indicates that this covenantal obligation included all future generations of Israel.

In the fourth chapter of the book, Mordecai is certain that God will preserve the Jews, as is evident from his words to Esther, "if you fail to speak up now, relief and deliverance will come to the Jews from a different direction." The reason he is confident of this is because of God's faithfulness to his covenant. But he also warns her, "but you and your father's family will perish" and "who knows whether you didn't come into your royal position precisely for such a time as this." Failure to embrace her responsibilities and to do what she could would have disastrous effects for her time and context. The same will be true for us. We too are responsible to do all we can to preserve Jewish communal continuity, for if we do not act, then there will be grave consequences to our inaction. And any approach to outreach among Jews that is indifferent to or disrupts or destroys Jewish communal cohesion is wrong.

CONCLUSION

We began by considering how Messianic Jewish leaders are lamenting the disparity between the stature of our movement in the purposes of God and a certain inertia evident among us. All of this seems so out of sync with our calling to be a sign, demonstration, and catalyst of God's consummating purposes for Israel. Many, if not most, will agree that it is now time for holy doubt. It is time for us to doubt that what we have is all there is. And it is time for us to doubt that we can ever live up to our movement's holy calling unless we prayerfully and wholeheartedly embrace and embody the agenda of the Son of David. It is time for us to energetically recruit others of our people to our Messiah's agenda, making Jewish disciples of the Son of David, who will live as Jews and pursue and promote his agenda until he comes.

It is time to enlist as ambassadors for the Kingdom of the Son of David, as recruiters for the Son of David and his agenda. Our message is more holistic than the message of individual soul salvation we have long proclaimed, which neglected the broader context of Yeshua's identity and agenda as the Son of David. This message to which we are being called is truly good news for the Jewish people, with implications for all nations and the entire created order. We could summarize our message and calling this way:

- The Messiah has come and he is coming again. His name is Yeshua, and he is the best possible news for the Jewish people.

- Through Yeshua the Son of David, the God of Israel—who has been with the Jewish people in all their afflictions—has come to rescue us again in greater manner and greater measure than ever before, as the prophets said he would (including talk of the atonement, the resurrection of Yeshua and its connection to the resurrection of the dead, of Israel as a nation (Ezekiel 37), of the Gentile world from the grave of idolatry, and Israel's full restoration as outlined in the New Messianic Jewish/Son of David Agenda).

- In him, all of God's promises to the Jewish people are being fulfilled.

- Come join with us, serving the God of Israel by advancing his agenda for his people in the context of Torah obedience and allegiance to Yeshua, the Son of David.

Serving the Son of David means more than simply saving Jewish souls. It means bringing our people into conformity with God's will as members of that covenant people who will someday all honor the Son of David as beneficiaries of his agenda's consummation. It means aligning ourselves and our people with God's future for all Israel.

I, Yeshua, have sent my angel to give you this testimony for the Messianic communities. I am the Root and Offspring of David, the bright Morning Star. The Spirit and the Bride say, 'Come!' Let anyone who hears say, 'Come!' And let anyone who is thirsty come—let anyone who wishes, take the water of life free of charge. . . . The one who is testifying to these things says, "Yes, I am coming soon!" Amen! Come, Lord Yeshua! (Rev 22:16–17, 20).

The Son of David comes. Isn't it time for the Messianic Jewish Congregational Movement to call out to him, "Lord, open our eyes," that he might heal our vision? Isn't it time to make these words our own, from *L'cha Dodi,* in our *Kabbalat Shabbat* liturgy?

Shake yourself off, from the dust! Put on your clothes of glory, my people, through the son of Jesse the Bethlehemite.[53]

Yes, it is time, indeed, it is past time. Urgently, and with all the energy that he inspires within us, we must rise up now, not some time in a far-off future, but now, shaking off old identities and paradigms, clothed in the glorious garments of the Son of David's Agenda, making it our own and ourselves his own until he comes.

The Son of David comes! May he find us serving no agenda but his.

---

53 "L'cha Dodi," *The Koren Siddur* (American Edition), Introduction, translation, and commentary by Rabbi Sir Jonathan Sacks. Jerusalem, Israel: Koren Publishers, Ltd., 2009, 320.

Printed in Great Britain
by Amazon.co.uk, Ltd.,
Marston Gate.